CAPTAIN PERFECTION

& THE SECRET OF SELF-COMPASSION

A SELF-HELP BOOK FOR
THE YOUNG PERFECTIONIST

JULIAN REEVE
ILLUSTRATED BY CAROL GREEN

Captain Perfection
& the Secret of Self-Compassion

Published by Buddha Perfect, LLC

B U D D H A
PERFECT

ISBN 978-1-7361976-8-4 (Paperback edition)
ISBN 978-1-7361976-0-8 (Ebook edition)

Library of Congress Control Number: 2020923205

www.julianreeve.com
www.captain-perfection.com

Illustrations by Carol Green
Stories Edited by Jenny Bowman

Dedicated to Louis, Gabe, Kyle, Oona Mae, Layla, Mason, Gabriel, and Darby

Special thanks to

Carol Green & Jenny Bowman, Lisa Donmall-Reeve,
Kymberlee Weil & Mark Sylvester, Michael Klein,
Steve White, & John Mader

Hi, I'm Captain Perfection!

Do you need everything to be perfect all of the time? Do you get angry or upset when you make mistakes? Do you find it hard to start something because you might not complete it perfectly? If this sounds like you, you might be a perfectionist.

A perfectionist is someone who aims for perfection in everything they do. They might say things like...

- ☐ I always want to be the best I can be
- ☐ I'm determined to do well
- ☐ I'm persistent and focused
- ☐ I pay great attention to detail in my work
- ☐ I'm motivated
- ☐ I always work hard
- ☐ I'm very well organized

These are all examples of *Healthy Perfectionism.* Healthy perfectionists have a tendency to do well in what they set out to accomplish because their determination to work hard and be the best helps them achieve very high standards.

Unfortunately, healthy perfectionism is often accompanied by *Unhealthy Perfectionism.* Perfectionists who experience unhealthy perfectionism will say things like...

☐ I often think about the mistakes I've made.

☐ I'm not happy if I don't achieve my goals.

☐ I find it hard to celebrate when I do well.

☐ I'm often hard on myself when I make mistakes.

☐ I often think there is only one way to do things.

☐ I won't finish a task unless it's going to be perfect.

☐ I think something is perfect or worthless, there's no in-between.

☐ I sometimes skip eating or sleeping so I can keep working on a project.

☐ I have a habit of setting unrealistic targets.

☐ I'm scared of failing/messing up.

☐ I sometimes feel anxious or depressed.

☐ I struggle to get things done on time.

☐ I often feel that others are better than me.

☐ I avoid doing things when I might fail.

Do you find yourself saying any of these things? Tick the box next to each phrase that sounds like you.

How many did you tick? If you ticked boxes in the healthy and unhealthy perfectionism lists, you're not alone.

Most perfectionists experience a combination of healthy and unhealthy perfectionism.

Did you know?

Over 30% of the world's population are estimated to be affected by perfectionism.

That's more than *2 BILLION* people!

If *you're* a perfectionist, you're not alone

Managing perfectionism

To be happy and to do well in life, perfectionists need to develop reliable ways to control their perfectionism.

Healthy perfectionism

The healthy part of your perfectionism doesn't need much management at all. You will naturally want to strive to be the very best you can be in everything you do.

Unhealthy perfectionism

The unhealthy part of perfectionism is different. It can cause us many problems and lead to low self-esteem. Low self-esteem occurs when we think we're not good enough, even though we are. This can make us really worried and anxious and can even lead to depression or physical issues with our bodies. There are many issues connected to unhealthy perfectionism, and that's why it's so important to develop ways to control it.

The self-compassion superpower!

One of the most effective ways to control unhealthy perfectionism is to use something called *self-compassion*. Self-compassion is 'the art of being kind to yourself' and it's really useful to use when our unhealthy perfectionism makes us feel angry or upset.

Self-compassion comes in three parts. *

#1 – Self-kindness

#2 – Mindfulness

#3 – Common Humanity

Let's look at these more closely...

#1 - **Self-kindness**

Self-kindness means to be as kind to yourself as you would be to others. Instead of being overly critical of yourself when you make mistakes, you offer yourself encouragement and support by being more forgiving of your mistake.

#2 - **Mindfulness**

Mindfulness means to be aware of what you are feeling in the present moment. It enables you to connect with 'now' rather than the past or the future. When you're mindful, you become focused on what you can see, feel, smell and hear in the present moment. Mindfulness helps to distract you from your unhealthy perfectionism and negative thoughts and feelings.

#3 – **Common Humanity**

Common Humanity is when you recognize that no-one is perfect and that everyone makes mistakes. It's learning to accept that we are all the same, and that it's completely normal for things to go wrong and for things not to be perfect all of the time.

*   definition by Kristin Neff, PhD

Happy perfectionists think of self-compassion as their SUPERPOWER!

Storytime!

Now we've learned about perfectionism and self-compassion, we need to understand more about when we might experience them. Let's read about three young perfectionists, Jack, Alexis and Noah, to see how I helped them use self-kindness, mindfulness, and compassion to overcome their unhealthy perfectionism.

Jack

Jack woke up feeling excited. Today was Wednesday, and that meant art class with Mr. Baxter, Jack's favorite teacher.

Jack liked to arrive early so he could prepare his desk properly, and today was no different. He neatly organized his pastels and pencils and waited patiently for his teacher.

"Today we will be drawing volcanoes," said Mr. Baxter.

Jack loved volcanoes! He'd been obsessed with them ever since he'd hiked around a real volcano in Hawaii with his family last summer.

Jack wanted his drawing to look perfect and started to build a picture of the volcano in his mind.

He decided that he'd make his volcano look just like the one in Hawaii , brown on the outside with some red bubbling lava on the inside. He took out his paper and began to draw.

Jack took his time getting the outside of his volcano looking the best it could. When he was happy with it, he moved on to draw the inside. As he reached for the red pencil to add the lava, he noticed Olivia's picture on the desk beside him.

Olivia had drawn little lava trails coming down from the side of her volcano and smoke was billowing from the top of the crater. Her drawing looked perfect.

Jack glanced back at his drawing. He hated it. *My volcano looks nothing like Olivia's,* thought Jack. Mine looks terrible! Jack felt his stomach get tight and his head start to ache.

Frustrated, he ripped the paper from his table and scrunched up his drawing. "I can't do it!" he said and burst into tears.

"What's the matter, Jack?" asked Mr. Baxter.

"I can't get my volcano to look as good as I want it to," he said.

"Let's see," said Mr. Baxter. He picked up Jack's drawing and uncrumpled the paper. "This looks really good!" he said. "What's wrong with it?"

"Everything!" replied Jack. He sunk his head in his hands. "It's not right. Everyone else's looks perfect."

Mr. Baxter asked Jack to try another drawing, but Jack refused. If his volcano wasn't going to be perfect, there wasn't any point in drawing it. He wished there was a way to stop feeling bad when he thought his work wasn't perfect, but he didn't know how. It seemed like Mr. Baxter didn't know either.

For the first time ever, Jack couldn't wait for art class to end.

The next Wednesday, Jack woke up dreading going to art class. He was worried that his work wouldn't be as good as Olivia's, and he didn't want to get upset again like last week.

He arrived at class early as usual but was surprised to see all the art materials packed away. Instead, a special guest was stood at the front of the room — and

he was dressed like a superhero!

"Class, I would like to introduce you to a good friend of mine," said Mr. Baxter. He glanced towards Jack, smiling. "Meet Captain Perfection!"

Whoa! thought Jack, admiring the costume. *I wonder what makes him perfect?*

"Hello everyone," said Captain Perfection. "My friends call me CP. How's everyone doing?"

"Hello CP!" yelled Jack, along with some of the other students.

"I'm here because I heard you could use my help," said CP. "How many of you like things to be perfect?"

Jack raised his hand and was surprised to see a lot of his friends doing the same.

"That could mean you're a perfectionist," said CP, and Jack nodded. He had heard this word before. Jack's mom had told him that he might be a perfectionist a few months ago. She had encouraged him to try and be happy with being really good at things rather than always trying to be perfect, but Jack found that really hard to do.

"How many of you compare your work with others, and sometimes think that other people's work is better than yours?" asked CP. Jack raised his hand. This was the exact same thing he had been so upset about the week before.

"Even though we all do it, and even though it will be hard not to, we really shouldn't compare ourselves with others. It's not good for us," said CP.

"Why not?" asked Jack. "I like to compare to see if I'm doing things right."

"I bet sometimes you feel bad when you make those comparisons, though," said CP.

Jack nodded. He never felt very good after he made comparisons.

"Our work is not meant to be like everyone else's because we are all unique and special people," said CP. "We all have our own individual talents and just because your drawing doesn't look like someone else's, that doesn't mean it's bad. We also need to remember that everyone has a different idea of what being perfect actually is. Some people might think that one thing is perfect, when others don't," said CP. "Let me show you."

CP held up a slightly crumpled piece of paper with a volcano on it. Jack immediately recognized it as his drawing from the week before. Mr. Baxter must have kept it!

"Hands up, who thinks this picture is perfect?" CP asked. Virtually the whole class put their hands up and Jack was amazed!

"One of you drew this," said CP. "Jack, where are you?"

Jack was so busy trying to figure out why his friends would think his drawing was perfect, he didn't hear CP call his name. His friend Justin nudged him in the ribs.

Jack got the message, and all the students cheered as he stood! Jack smiled, shyly.

"Your classmates think your work is really good, but I hear you weren't very happy with it?" said CP.

"I got upset because my volcano wasn't as good as Olivia's," said Jack, feeling slightly embarrassed.

"So, you were comparing?" asked CP.

"Yes," said Jack.

"Did you try as hard as you could to get your picture as good as it could be?" asked CP.

"Yes," Jack said again.

"Then you should be really proud and happy with your work, because doing your very best is always enough. As we just saw, we all have a different idea of what a perfect volcano looks like, so we owe it to ourselves to be true to our own vision and not compare with others," CP said. "What do you think you could do differently next time?"

Jack thought hard about CP's question before answering. "If I concentrate on doing my best work, then I won't be busy comparing it to others."

CP smiled. "That's right. Aiming to be the very best you can be is a good thing, but if you feel that it's not quite your best work, you must to be kind to yourself instead of getting frustrated or angry."

"How?" asked Jack.

"The next time you're drawing a picture and you feel yourself getting frustrated or starting to compare, I'd like you to do two things. First, I want you to stop what you're doing and take a deep breath in, and then let a deep breath out — like this." CP slowly breathed in through his nose, and out through his mouth.

"You should feel your belly getting bigger when you breathe in and smaller again when you breathe out. Try it with me," CP said to the class. Jack and his friends breathed in slowly through their nose and out through their mouth, once, twice, then three times, feeling their bellies getting bigger and smaller each time.

"Nice work!" said CP. "Now, when you're doing this, I'd like you to look around the room and make a mental note of everything you see. You might see a chair, or a desk, or a blackboard or some books. Note them all down in your head. Try it with me now," said CP.

Jack continued with his breathing and looked around the room. He noticed the curtains, lights, carpet and coats before CP spoke again. "What we're doing here is practicing Mindfulness. By focusing on our breathing and making a note of what's in the room with us, we're keeping our mind focused in the present. When we do this, we stop doing unhealthy things like comparing our work to others, and we're able to look at our own work through kind eyes. Pretty cool, right?!"

Jack nodded, eagerly. It seemed like a fun way to stay focused on his own picture the next time he was drawing.

"Remember," said CP, "you're all very special people, with unique gifts and talents. You're not meant to be like anyone else, and so there's no need to compare yourselves to others."

The bell rang for break time, and Mr. Baxter thanked CP before taking a photo of the class with their new friend. Jack left the class smiling. He was happy to have learned new ways to avoid getting upset when things weren't quite perfect.

The next week in art class, Mr. Baxter asked the students to draw a picture of the Moon. Jack was sitting next to Scott, who was really good at art.

The students were all working happily when suddenly Jack started to compare. *Scott's Moon looks really good,* thought Jack. Mine is nowhere near as good as his.

Jack felt his stomach get tight and his head started to ache. He felt his frustration rising when he remembered what CP had taught him.

Breathe in slowly through the nose, and out through the mouth. Jack did this once, twice, then three times. He then began to look around the room noticing what was there. As he looked his stomach started to relax and the tension left his head. CP's advice was working! Jack looked around the room until he became calmer.

Feeling better, Jack turned back to his own picture. He decided that his drawing wasn't bad after all, and that it deserved to be finished. Jack picked up his pencil to finish his own, unique, drawing.

As he drew, Jack suddenly realized what it was that made CP so perfect. He was kind to himself!

When his picture was finished, Jack held it up feeling proud of his work. Not only had he used mindfulness to succeed, but he'd chosen to view his work with kind eyes.

What have we learned?

- You are not alone — some of your friends might be perfectionists, too.

- We shouldn't compare ourselves to others, because we are unique, and our work is not meant to be like everyone else's.

- If you feel yourself getting frustrated or starting to compare, remember the exercises CP taught to the class.

- Always be kind to yourself when trying to be the best you can be.

- If you're struggling with your perfectionism, tell your parents or a teacher.

CP says...

If you're like Jack and sometimes get angry or upset whenever you haven't done your best work, it's important to try and be aware of your feelings.

If you...

• Start to feel hot and sweaty

• Feel your heart start to beat faster than normal

• Think that things are getting noisy in your head

...these are signs that you might be about to get upset. When you feel these things, try and focus on the exercises I taught to Jack. The more you practice, the better you will become at catching yourself before your emotions get out of control.

Be gentle with yourself. You are an amazing person, and you deserve to be happy!

Alexis

"Slow down, slow down! You're walking way too quickly," Emily yelled to her best friend, Alexis. Her dog, Ollie, barked in agreement.

"Sorry," said Alexis, slowing down. "I'm just anxious to get home and start my assignment."

"I don't know why you have to rush home for that," said Emily. "It's obvious you'll get an A — you always get an A!"

Alexis laughed. Emily was right, she regularly got perfect grades on her homework. She was always careful to make sure that every little detail was accurate and flawless before handing it in.

"Maybe," said Alexis, "but I'm not very good at Geography. I'm going to need lots of time to finish the take-home test."

Emily rolled her eyes. "Why do you always think you're not very good at stuff?" she asked. "You're the brainiest kid at school!"

Alexis shrugged, but secretly knew the answer.

She was a perfectionist, and perfectionists often think they're not good enough at school, even if they are.

They arrived at Emily's house, and Ollie jumped up for one last pat on the head from Alexis. The two girls hugged goodbye, and Alexis hurried home.

Alexis's bedroom was immaculate. She kept all of her belongings laid out very neatly and knew exactly where everything was. Her wall was covered with pictures of her friends from school. Alexis had a lot of friends. She was certain that everyone liked her because her grades were perfect. Why else would they want to be her friend?

Alexis unpacked her school bag and opened the test. "Time to be perfect!" she said, trying to muster her best self. Alexis read the first question.

'Question 1: Name the longest river in the USA.' That's easy, thought Alexis. *It's the Mississippi.* She wrote down her answer and moved on to question two.

'*Which one of these cities is the capital of Texas – Austin, Dallas, Houston, San Antonio?*' *Hmmm,* Alexis thought to herself. *I think it's Austin, but it might be Dallas.* Alexis took her time to think. She wasn't quite sure about this one.

While she was thinking, she noticed all her friends in the photos on the wall. *I have to be perfect,* she thought. *They won't want to be my friends otherwise.* Her heart seemed to beat faster as she thought about not being liked.

Alexis sat for ages thinking. *Tick, tock, tick, tock* went the clock on the wall. "Austin," Alexis finally said out loud, before writing down her answer.

She was just about to move on to question three, when something made Alexis doubt her answer to question one. *Wait,* she thought. *Isn't the longest river in the U.S. the Missouri River?* Alexis thought back to a TV show she'd watched a few months ago on big rivers but couldn't recall which one was the longest. I have to be perfect! she thought.

Alexis looked again at the photos on the wall and her heart began to race. She reached for her computer for help but remembered that she'd been instructed not to look up the answers on the internet. *Tick, tock, tick, tock* went the clock on the wall. Alexis's palms and forehead felt sticky as she wrestled with the two choices. *Tick, tock, tick, tock.* Finally, she decided that it must be the Missouri and wrote that down before forcing herself to move on.

'Question 3: What is Earth's largest continent - Antarctica, Asia, Africa, or Europe?' Alexis was convinced the answer was Asia, but something told her that it might be Africa. *Tick, tock, tick, tock* went the clock on the wall. She sat at her desk for ages thinking about her answer and began to feel really anxious. *I have to be perfect!* she thought, looking once again at the photos of her friends. Back and forth she went trying to decide the correct answer. *Tick, tock, tick, tock.* Eventually she decided on Asia.

She was just about to start question four when
Alexis heard her dad calling upstairs. "Time for bed,
Alexis."

Alexis looked at the clock on the wall. "Nine
o'clock?!" she gasped. "It can't be that late already, I've

only answered three of the questions!" Alexis started to panic, not quite knowing what to do.

She looked through the rest of the test and saw there were seven questions left. She quickly read each one and added the first answer that came into her head. Alexis felt terrible. She'd never run out of time on her homework before — what was happening?! She was desperate to spend more time on each question, but really needed to get ready for bed. Her dad would check in on her soon and wouldn't be happy if she was still working. *I'll check these answers again in the morning,* she promised herself as she went to brush her teeth.

The next day, Alexis found herself in a rush. She'd woken up slightly later than usual and was now struggling to make it to school on time. She threw her test into her bag and grabbed a piece of toast before racing out the door.

Alexis arrived at her classroom with one minute to spare. She'd made it! Her teacher, Miss Pantry, was walking round the room collecting the student's homework assignments. *Oh, no!* thought Alexis. *I haven't had time to check my answers!*

"You'll get your grades tomorrow," said Miss Pantry. Alexis handed in her test and spent the rest of the day worrying. It was far from her usual perfect work.

The next day Alexis arrived at school feeling nervous. She hadn't been able to sleep much because she was convinced that her friends would stop liking her if her grades were anything less than perfect.

As she got to her place, Alexis noticed that Miss Pantry had put each pupil's marked homework on their desks already, and that some of her friends were looking at her and whispering. *What's going on?* she thought.

Alexis picked up her homework. She'd been given a C! *What?!* It was her first C ever. Alexis slumped down on her chair. She felt like crying but wouldn't allow herself to get upset with her friends in the room.

Alexis looked through the test. Five of her ten answers had been wrong, including the question about the rivers. It had been the Mississippi all along! Alexis heard some laughter from the front of the class. One of her friends had been given an A and everyone was congratulating her. Alexis wanted the ground to open up and swallow her, she was so embarrassed. *How could I have let this happen?* she screamed inside, over and over.

After what felt like the longest Geography lesson in history, Alexis ran to a quiet corner of the school yard and began to cry. She felt like her heart might actually break, she was so upset. "I can't believe I got a C!" she said and banged her fists on the wall.

"Alexis, what's wrong?" It was Emily.

Alexis wiped her eyes and faced her best friend. "I got a C on my test," she said through her tears. "This has never happened before. No-one will like me now."

"Wait," said Emily, "do you think I only like you because you get A's on your homework?"

Alexis thought about Emily's question. She knew

that Emily was different from her other friends, but why

would Emily want to be friends with her if her grades weren't perfect? Slightly embarrassed, Alexis nodded.

"Well I don't think that, OK?" said Emily. "I like you because you're awesome and you like to hang out with me and Ollie, and we have fun together!"

Alexis stopped crying for a second.

"Really?" she asked, willing the answer to be true.

"Of course!" said Emily.

Alexis started to calm down. Maybe she should talk to Emily about her perfectionism. Maybe Emily would understand. "Do you ever feel the need to be perfect?" she asked.

"No," replied Emily, "which is just as well because I never am!"

Alexis giggled, but remained serious. "I wish I could be like that," she said. "But I can't. I'm a perfectionist."

"I'm sorry, Alexis. How can I help you?" Emily asked.

"I'm not sure, really," replied Alexis.

Emily felt sorry for Alexis. Being a perfectionist looked like very hard work. She vowed to do whatever she could do to help her friend.

That night the two girls took Ollie out for his walk after dinner as usual. On the way home, Emily led them on a slight detour via a very pretty street that was lined with trees. At the end of the street was a yellow house. It was big and old, but it wasn't falling down. The house had been lovingly restored, and Alexis thought the gardens looked perfect.

"Woah," said Alexis. "This house looks like it's out of a magazine. I wonder who lives here?"

Emily smiled, knowingly. "A friend of mine. Come on!"

As they approached the front door, Ollie's tail started wagging. He seemed excited to see whoever was inside. Emily rang the bell, and in no time at all, a man appeared wearing a funny costume.

"Hello Emily," said the man.

"Hi CP!" Emily replied. She stepped back so she could introduce her two friends. "Alexis, meet Captain Perfection," she said.

"Hi," said Alexis, nervously.

"My friends call me CP," said Captain Perfection, shaking Alexis's hand.

"CP is a friend of my brothers," said Emily. "They've been working together on his perfectionism." CP smiled and asked how her brother was doing before inviting them inside. "Please, come in!" he said.

Inside Ollie immediately trotted into the kitchen to find CP's dog. "Don't eat Griffin's food!" said Emily, and CP laughed.

"Emily tells me you had a problem with a Geography test," CP said to Alexis.

"Yes, that's right. I got a C because I ran out of time to finish it properly," said Alexis, feeling embarrassed.

"What made you run out of time?" asked CP.

"I was taking too long trying to be perfect with each answer," Alexis replied.

CP smiled. "You know that most perfectionists struggle with this, right? It's not just you."

Alexis didn't know that, and suddenly felt a bit lighter.

"Here's a great trick to always make sure you finish a test or assignment on time," said CP. "Let's say you've just answered the first question in a test, and your perfectionism tells you that your answer might be wrong—"

"That's exactly what happened to me on the question about the rivers!" Alexis cut in.

"Well," continued CP, "you have two options. You can either spend a lot of time trying to figure out whether your first answer is correct or not, or you can manage your perfectionism better by saying 'my answer is good enough for now' and then move on."

"But if I don't go back and check, how will I know

that what I've done is perfect?" asked Alexis.

"Go back and check at the end. As you're doing your assignment, write down which question your perfectionism is telling you might be wrong, and once you've finished the assignment — and only then — go back and check off as much of the list as you have time for." Alexis nodded. CP's advice was making sense.

"Remember," said CP, "just because your perfectionism tells you that an answer isn't correct, that doesn't mean to say that the answer is wrong. You have a choice of whether to listen to your perfectionism or not."

Alexis thought about what CP said. If she had not let her perfectionism question her first answer about the rivers, she would have gotten that question right. "Thanks, CP," she said. "I'll try this in my next assignment."

Alexis suddenly remembered how much better she felt after talking to Emily about her perfectionism.

Maybe asking CP to help her stop panicking when she felt she needed to be perfect was a good idea?

"Is there anything I can do to stay calm when I'm worried that I'm not going to be perfect?" asked Alexis.

CP smiled. "Have you ever heard of a mantra?" Alexis shook her head.

"A mantra is a phrase that we repeat over and over when we need to calm ourselves down and feel better about ourselves."

Alexis smiled at Emily. This sounded like it was going to be really useful!

"Try saying this phrase," said CP. "If I always try my best, I will always be enough."

"If I always try my best, I will always be enough," said Alexis. It felt good.

"Now say it ten times," said CP. "Why is it important to say it ten times?" asked Emily. Alexis was wondering the same.

"What we're practicing here is called 'self-kindness'," said CP. "You're reminding yourself that you are unique and special, and saying it over and over helps you start believing what you're saying. Let's close our eyes and say it all together."

Alexis reached for Emily's hand as they started to speak. "If I always try my best, I will always be enough," said the girls, ten times. As they finished, they opened their eyes.

"I'm glad you brought your friend to see me," CP said to Emily. "It's always important to talk about our perfectionism if it's causing us problems."

"Anything for a real friend," said Emily, smiling at Alexis, who was feeling very relaxed. As the girls and Ollie walked home, Alexis felt grateful.

"I'm glad I told you about being a perfectionist," she said to Emily, "and thank you for introducing me to CP."

"No problem! I hope he helps you." Emily paused for a minute. "I was thinking about what you said to me earlier — about thinking you have to be perfect for your friends." Alexis nodded. "If anyone stops liking you because you didn't get an A, you might want to consider if they are actually a real friend or not. Real friends don't care about grades, they care about the person you are."

Emily stopped walking and turned to Alexis. "It's virtually impossible for people to get A-grades all the time," she said. "Human beings are not built to be perfect, they are meant to get things wrong so they can learn from their mistakes and be even better afterwards."

Alexis was struck by the power of Emily's words. It felt good. She could feel it in her stomach. "When did you become so wise?" she asked.

Emily laughed. "I'm not sure if I'm wise — I've just learned a lot from my brother's experience, I guess."

They hugged each other and Alexis suddenly felt tired. What a day this had been! Emily had shown Alexis that she didn't need to be perfect for her friends to like her, and with CP's help, she now knew how to manage her perfectionism whenever it caused her to second guess herself.

Alexis smiled at her best friend. "You're a real friend, you know, and I feel lucky to have you."

Emily smiled. "You too," she said, before taking Alexis's hand to walk back home. Ollie wagged his tail and barked in approval.

What have we learned?

- Always get to the end of an assignment or test before going back to check on your answers.

- Sometimes your perfectionism will trick you into thinking your answers are wrong, when they aren't.

- If your friends need you to be perfect, they're probably not real friends.

- Real friends will like you because of who you are, not the grades you get.

- We can't get A grades all of the time. Human beings are not meant to be perfect. Everybody makes mistakes, and that's OK.

- If you're struggling with your perfectionism, tell your parents, teacher or a friend.

CP says ...

It's really important that we remember how special we are. Part of the reason Alexis felt that her friends wouldn't like her if she didn't get perfect grades is that she'd forgotten that what she has to offer the world was much more than being good at school.

Remind yourself of the things that make you unique and do it often. You're amazing!

Noah

Noah was at the piano practicing for his big concert on Friday night. He loved playing the piano, especially his own one at home. His mom had rented it from the local music store, and although it was old and scratched and not quite perfect, Noah thought it was the best piano he'd ever played.

Der, dum-dum, der, dum-dum, fiddle de-deeee the music tinkled. Noah had been practicing really hard for weeks. He wanted his performance to be perfect for his mom who was going to be in the audience.

Der, dum-dum, der, dum-dum, fiddle de-deeeee. Der, dum-dum, der, dum-dum, CRASH! Noah played a wrong note. He sighed loudly and banged the keys with his hands. He hated it when he made mistakes. In fact, making mistakes was his least favorite thing in the world. "Let's try that again," he said, feeling frustrated.

Der, dum-dum, der, dum-dum, fiddle de-deeeee. Der, dum-dum, der, dum-dum, CRASH! Noah made the same mistake!

What are you doing? he said to himself. *You know this piece really well — come on, you can do better!* Noah was always hard on himself when he made mistakes, especially when he was trying to make his mom proud. He had to be perfect.

Der, dum-dum, der, dum-dum, fiddle de-deeeee the music played. *Der, dum-dum, der, dum-dum, CRASH!* Noah made the same mistake again. "Why can't I play it?" he screamed. He slammed the lid of the piano down and stormed upstairs to his bedroom.

Noah threw himself on his bed. He didn't understand why he was making mistakes when he knew the piece so well, and he was embarrassed to be messing up when his mom could hear him.

"What's all the fuss about?" Noah's mom was at the bedroom door.

"I can't get it right" said Noah, through his tears.

"It sounded good to me" said his mom. Noah could tell she was trying to cheer him up.

"I'm just not good enough," he said.

"Don't worry honey, you'll get it right next time," she said, trying to encourage him.

Noah wasn't listening. *She doesn't understand,* he thought. *What if I don't get it right? What if it isn't perfect? It's nice that Mom believes in me, but what if I fail? Will she still be proud of me?*

That night, Noah tossed and turned in his sleep. He was dreaming he was at the school concert making lots of mistakes in his performance. *Der, dum, CRASH, Der, dum, CRASH, fiddle de-CRASH* went the music. Laughs rose up from the audience with each wrong note, and he could see his mom frowning and looking worried. *Der, dum, CRASH, Der, dum, CRASH.* He knew the right notes, but he couldn't play them. Noah was so embarrassed. All he wanted to do was run off stage.

Suddenly, Noah woke up in a sweat. "Oh, thank goodness," he said out loud when he realized it was a dream. Noah took a few deep breaths and had a sip of water to try and calm himself down. He tried to go back to sleep but couldn't stop worrying. *What if his dream came true? What if he made mistakes during the real concert? Would his mom still be proud of him?* Noah was really tired, but his mind wouldn't stop racing. He tossed and turned for most of the night and didn't sleep much at all.

The next day, Noah was exhausted. He was so tired he managed to pull on odd socks when he was getting dressed and was nearly late for school because his mom had made him go and change.

"Noah, what's going on, honey? I'm worried you're pushing yourself too hard at the piano," his mom said in the car.

"I just need to practice a little more, Mom. I'll be OK," said Noah, who wasn't at all convinced by his answer.

Noah spent the day worrying about his dream. He couldn't focus in his lessons and didn't learn much at all. He couldn't wait for the school day to end so he could get back to his piano.

After school, Noah raced home. He flung open the door to find his mom visiting with a friend.

"I want you to meet my friend, Captain Perfection," Mom said.

Noah smiled and shook Captain Perfection's hand.

"You can call me CP," he said. "I hear you have a big concert coming up?"

"This Friday," said Noah, "and I need to practice."

"Okay honey, go right ahead," said Noah's mom. "CP and I will be in the kitchen if you need anything."

Noah managed a quick nod and made his way to the piano. *Der, dum-dum, der, dum-dum, fiddle de-deeeee* the music tinkled. *Der, dum-dum, CRASH!* Noah had made another mistake. Feeling slightly panicked, he went back to the beginning of the piece and started again. *Der, dum-dum, Der, dum-CRASH!* Another mistake. "Why am I so useless?" he shouted and buried his head in his hands.

Captain Perfection had been listening through the door and joined Noah in the living room. "How's the practice going, Noah?" he asked.

"Not very well," Noah replied, sullenly. "I've been practicing for days, and I should be able to play this piece perfectly by now."

"You look tired. Are you sleeping OK?" CP asked.

"Usually I sleep well," replied Noah, "but last night I had a dream that I was making mistakes in the school concert. I couldn't get back to sleep because I was worrying that I wouldn't be perfect on Friday."

"Why do you feel like you have to be perfect?" asked CP. Noah whispered so his mom wouldn't hear. "Because if I am, my mom will be proud of me, and I like it when she's proud of me."

CP smiled. "I'm sure your mom will be very proud of you whether you are perfect or not," he whispered back.

Noah felt his cheeks turn red.

"Do you think your mom would even notice if you made a mistake at the concert?" CP asked Noah.

"Yes!" he replied. *Didn't CP understand?* "Everyone will. It'll be really obvious if I screw up!"

"May I?" CP asked, sliding onto the piano bench. He started playing a well-known piece of classical

music. "You know this piece, right?" he asked as he
played.

"Yes," said Noah.

"OK," said CP, "I want you to stop me when I make
a mistake".

Did-dle did-dle da da da, did-dle did-dle daa went the music. *Did-dle did-dle CRASH!* CP played a wrong note on purpose, but Noah didn't stop him. CP kept playing. *Did-dle did-dle dee Did- CRASH!* CP played another wrong note, but still Noah didn't stop him. CP added another wrong note in the next phrase, but Noah *still* didn't realize what was happening. CP stopped playing.

"Well?" CP asked.

"Well, what?!" asked Noah.

CP laughed. "I've played three wrong notes already!"

Noah was confused. "Really?! I didn't hear them."

"So, if you didn't hear them, do you think it's possible that your mom wouldn't notice a mistake in the concert?" CP asked.

"I guess so," replied Noah, thoughtfully. "Perfectionists will always notice when they make a mistake, but that doesn't mean to say that everyone else will," said CP. "There are many times when we think we're imperfect, but nobody else does.

"If you do make a mistake, it's important to remember that being hard on ourselves and making ourselves feel bad isn't good for us," CP continued. "Being angry and frustrated isn't healthy for our minds or our bodies, so we must be gentle with ourselves when we make mistakes, OK? It's called self-compassion."

"But how can I not feel bad about myself when I make a mistake?" Noah asked.

"Let me show you a trick," said CP. "The next time you make a mistake, notice that you've made it, but don't judge yourself for it. Remember that everybody makes mistakes, perfectionists just feel worse when they make one. Keep playing the music, and don't stop."

Noah nodded, trying to take everything in.

"Making mistakes is a part of life," CP continued. Everyone makes them, it's only human. It's called common humanity, and the people that love us, like our moms, understand this and will always love us no matter what."

Noah found himself feeling better. He was beginning to understand that being kind to himself when he made a mistake meant he would get less angry and frustrated.

"Why don't you try it now?" said CP, moving away from the piano. Noah sat down and started to play his piece. *Der, dum-dum, der, dumdum, fiddle de-deeeee. Der, dum-dum, CRASH!* Noah made a mistake, but instead of stopping and judging himself, he kept going.

Der, dum-dum, der, dum-dum, fiddle de-dee tinkled the music. As he played, Noah felt himself gain more confidence. *Der, dum-dum, Der, dum-dum, ta-da ta-da ta-da dee.* The longer he played the more focused he became, and before he knew it, he was at the end of the piece having made hardly any mistakes at all!

CP stood up and applauded. "Bravo, maestro!" he said. "That was wonderful!" Noah was thrilled. "Thanks, CP," he said, grateful for the help.

CP turned to leave Noah to his practice when he remembered something. "There's one more thing that every perfectionist should know," he said. Noah listened very carefully. "When we make mistakes, we have to let them go, because they are in the past. If we hold on to them, they affect our present and our future, and that's not healthy for us. That's why you couldn't sleep last night — you were dwelling on the past, allowing it to affect your present, and your future. Do you understand?"

"I do," replied Noah, smiling. Something about that made perfect sense. Noah thanked CP and sat back down to practice. This time he wouldn't worry about making a mistake because he knew exactly what to do if he did.

Friday's concert came around quickly, and Noah was nervous as he sat in the back of his mom's car on the way to the school.

"Good luck tonight, Noah," his mom said. "You'll be brilliant!"

"Thanks, Mom," said Noah, hoping she was right.

As they arrived at the school, Noah's mom remembered something CP had told her in the kitchen and said one last thing: "You know I'm proud of you, right?"

Noah was slightly startled. "But I haven't played my piece yet," he said.

"I don't need to hear your piece to be proud of you, Noah. I'm always proud of you, and whatever happens tonight, please know that you will always be good enough for me. I'm sorry if I don't say that as often as I should. I will from now on — I promise."

Noah got out of the car and gave his mom a big hug. "Thanks, Mom. I needed that."

Perhaps tonight's performance would be just fine after all.

What have we learned?

- It's OK to make mistakes.

- Everybody makes mistakes — perfectionists just feel worse when they make one.

- When you make a mistake in music, don't stop playing. Notice the mistake, don't judge yourself for it, and keep playing.

- When we make mistakes, we have to let them go. If we don't, they affect our present and our future, which isn't good for our minds and bodies.

- Perfectionists will always notice when they make a mistake, but that doesn't mean to say everyone else will.

- There are many times when we think we're imperfect, but nobody else does.

- If you are struggling with your perfectionism, talk to an adult. Remember that talking to your parents about it will make you feel better and gives them a chance to help you.

CP says...

Another way that Noah could have made himself feel better when he was making mistakes was to talk to his Mom.

Perfectionists often feel like they are alone, but that's not the case. If Noah had been brave and trusted that his Mom could help him, he wouldn't have gotten so frustrated or not been able to sleep.

Be brave and ask for help when you need it!

Build your own Superpower!

Now it's time to develop your very own superpower to defeat your unhealthy perfectionism!

But first, **Let's Visualize!**

Imagine you're playing a video game. The game is called *The Perfect Conquest,* and to win the game you have to defeat unhealthy perfectionism. You have three weapons you can use to win; selfkindness, mindfulness, and common humanity. Which one you use to fight unhealthy perfectionism will depend on the situation you are in.

Now that you know what you can achieve with self-kindness, mindfulness, and common humanity, can you see yourself winning the game?

Self-kindness combined with mindfulness and common humanity make up **self-compassion.**

Self-compassion is your SUPERPOWER!

Let's Build SELF-KINDNESS!

Do You Remember?

- Jack used **self-kindness** when he was drawing his Moon. He decided that his drawing deserved to be finished, and that comparing his work to others wasn't a good idea. He was kind to himself.

- Noah used **self-kindness** at the piano. Instead of judging himself each time he made a mistake, Noah learned to keep going with his music rather than stopping and giving himself a hard time.

- Alexis used **self-kindness** by reminding herself she didn't have to be perfect for her friends. She realized that her efforts to be perfect were stressing her out, and that real friends would like her even if she didn't get perfect grades.

Do you remember the mantra I taught to Alexis? "If I always do my best, I will always be good enough." Here are some other self-kindness mantras for you to use when you're experiencing unhealthy perfectionism.

Reminder: A mantra is a phrase that we repeat to ourselves over and over. We use a mantra when we experience low self-esteem and need to feel better about ourselves.

Try saying each one of these phrases slowly in your head. Repeat each phrase ten times.

- *I speak to myself with kindness and I treat myself with kindness*
- *I love myself; I believe in myself; I am enough*
- *Making mistakes is a part of life*

How do you feel?

Using a mantra is a great way to quieten the mind and feel calmer when our unhealthy perfectionism surfaces. Try saying a mantra the next time you feel yourself becoming angry or upset! Maybe try sitting like this when you say your mantra.

Let's Build MINDFULNESS!

Do You Remember?

· Jack used **mindfulness** when he started to get upset about Scott's moon. He recognized that he was starting to compare his drawing with Scott's and used mindfulness as a diversion tactic.

Let's try a mindfulness exercise similar to the one I taught to Jack!

· Lie flat on the floor with your eyes closed and your arms out by your side. Breathe deeply in and out a few times and try and relax every muscle in your body.

· When you're ready, use your imagination to take you to a place where you feel happy and safe. It might be far, far away, or it might be close to where you live. It might be an imaginary place! It doesn't matter.

· What does the place look like? Does it have hills and mountains or is it flat? Is it by the ocean or in a city? Are you inside or outside? What can you hear? What can you smell?

· Now imagine doing something really fun. You could fly a kite or run along the beach with your friends. You could hike to the top of the tallest mountain or play with the animals in the zoo.

- Now imagine you're hungry, so you find somewhere to eat your favorite food. What does it taste like?

- As you finish your food, be thankful for being in such a safe and happy place. Then, begin to return to the present.

- Open your eyes, take a deep breath in and out, and come back to the room.

How was that? It's fun, isn't it?!

The next time you find yourself comparing or thinking things like: *"I'm not as fast as…"*; *"My clothes are not as cool as…"*; *"My picture is not as creative as…"*; see how mindful you can be. Use all of your senses to stay focused on what's around you or what you're doing. It'll help keep your unhealthy perfectionism away. **Awesome!**

Let's Build COMMON HUMANITY!

Do You Remember?

- Alexis learned about **common humanity** when her friend Emily reminded her that humans aren't perfect and that everyone makes mistakes.

- Noah learned about **common humanity** when I taught him that we all make mistakes, perfectionists just feel worse when they make one.

Here's a common humanity exercise that we can do to help us with our unhealthy perfectionism. We need to do this sometime *after* our perfectionism has made us angry or upset, because common humanity is harder to practice when we experience perfectionism in the moment.

- Find a comfortable chair or sit cross-legged on the floor. Take a few deep breaths and allow your body to relax completely.

- Now, I'd like you to think about your best friend. What's their name? What do they look like? Visualize this person in your mind.

- Now imagine that you and your friend switch. You become them and they become you. Think back to the last time you got upset about your perfectionism and imagine your friend is in the same situation you were in. What might you say to them to help them feel better? Write a few things down. *You might say something like: "Don't worry — we all make mistakes" or "It's completely normal to make mistakes."*

- Think about how your friend must be feeling when they experience unhealthy perfectionism. What are they feeling? What else might you say to them to help them to feel better? Write down anything that comes to mind.

- Now take a deep breath in and out and come back to the room.

How was that for you?

Common Humanity is the realization that you're not alone with your perfectionism. It's understanding that it is completely normal to have the feelings you're having when you experience unhealthy perfectionism, and it's a reminder that you're not the only perfectionist in the world.

What words and phrases did you write down to describe what your friend was feeling? What did you say to help your friend feel better?

See if you can use some of these words and phrases for yourself the next time you experience unhealthy perfectionism!

Don't forget!

All of these exercises will take time to learn and get right. Be patient and persistent and keep practicing them whenever you can. Be kind to yourself! You probably won't get them right on the first try — and that's ok! If that happens, forgive yourself and try again.

When to use your Superpower

Congratulations! You've now built your new **Self-Compassion Superpower!** Now we need to do what Jack, Alexis, and Noah did, and learn *when* to use it.

Let's look again at the list of things that we might say when we experience unhealthy perfectionism:

- I often think about the mistakes I've made.
- I'm not happy if I don't achieve my goals.
- I find it hard to celebrate when I do well.
- I'm often hard on myself when I make mistakes.
- I often think there is only one way to do things.
- I won't finish a task unless it's going to be perfect.
- I think something is perfect or worthless, there's no in-between.
- I sometimes skip eating or sleeping so I can keep working on a project.
- I have a habit of setting unrealistic targets.
- I'm scared of failing/messing up.
- I sometimes feel anxious or depressed.
- I struggle to get things done on time.
- I often feel that others are better than me.
- I avoid doing things when I might fail.

Let's now look at which part of our new superpower we might use for each experience:

I often think about the mistakes I've made.

Mindfulness: Remember to stay present. Spending too much time in the past isn't healthy, and it affects our future.

Self-kindness: Forgive yourself for your mistakes.

I'm not happy if I don't achieve my goals.

Self-kindness: Check to see if your goals were realistic. If they weren't, change your goals to something you can achieve. If they were realistic, change your approach to achieving the goal.

I find it hard to celebrate when I do well.

Self-kindness: Perfectionists often move onto the next task as soon as they've finished the first one. Challenge yourself to celebrate your achievements before you move onto something new.

I'm often hard on myself when I make mistakes.

Self-kindness: Be gentle with yourself. The harder you are on yourself, the more likely it is that you will keep making mistakes.

Self-kindness: Take regular breaks so you can re-set and refocus.

Common humanity: Remind yourself that everyone makes mistakes, and that it's completely natural for that to happen.

I often think there is only one way to do things.

Self-kindness: Step back from what you're doing and look at it from someone else's point of view. Identify other ways to achieve your goal.

I won't finish a task unless it's going to be perfect.

Self-kindness: Don't be so hard on yourself! Remember that other people might think your work is really good and your work deserves to be finished.

Common humanity: Remind yourself that everyone makes mistakes and that it's completely normal to feel like you do.

I think something is perfect or worthless, there's no in-between.

Self-kindness: There is beauty in everything, even if you don't think it's perfect. Look at the thing you've created and write down all the good parts about it.

I sometimes skip eating or sleeping so I can keep working on a project.

Self-kindness: Remember that your work won't be good unless you look after your mind and body first. Take breaks regularly to get water and food when you need them. If you forget to take breaks, set a timer to remind you!.

I have a habit of setting unrealistic targets.

Self-kindness: Before you take action on any plan or project, check to see if the target you've set for yourself is realistic. Check the amount of time you need, and that all other parts of the projects are possible before you commit to your desired outcome. Adjust the expectation of your target if not.

I'm scared of failing/messing up.

Common humanity: Remember that everyone feels like this sometimes.

Self-kindness: Try to imagine how happy you would be if you succeeded. What does that feel like? Ask yourself: Is there any reason why I would fail? Very often our fear of failure is actually the fear of the unknown. Just because we don't know what the outcome will be, that doesn't mean to say we know we will fail. Go for it!

I sometimes feel anxious or depressed.

Self-kindness: Our body will often tell us what it needs to feel less anxious or depressed. Listen to it. If it needs rest, then rest. If it needs to eat, have some healthy food.

Common humanity: Remember that everyone feels like this sometimes. It's not just you and you are not alone. Reach out to a friend for some support.

I struggle to get things done on time.

Self-kindness: Don't fall into the trap of trying to make the first thing you do absolutely perfect. Get it to where it's 'good enough for now' and move on. Come back to make it as good as it can be once you've finished the project.

Common humanity: Remember that all perfectionists struggle with this. It's not just you, and you are not alone.

I often feel that others are better than me.

Self-kindness: Write down 5 things that are amazing about you. It can be anything. Focus on those things, not on your negative thoughts. You are AWESOME!

Common humanity: Remember that *everyone* feels like this sometimes.

I avoid doing things when I might fail.

Self-kindness: This is called procrastination. When you feel like this, look at what you are scared of failing at and break it down into small pieces. For example: if you're scared of failing at a school project, don't think of it as 'one big thing'. Break it down into a number of smaller sections, and create the complete project by finishing each small section as well as you can before moving on to the next.

CP's Pro Tips

- **#1** If you find it difficult to take breaks whilst you're working, set an alarm to remind you to take one!

- **#2** Try this MINDFULNESS technique to instantly forget about a mistake you just made... *when you've made a mistake, close your eyes and visualize two buttons on a machine; one reads SELECT, and the other DELETE. SELECT the mistake in your mind, and then DELETE it.* This is a really great way to stay in the present and forget about the past!

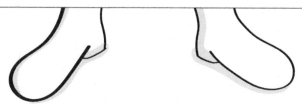

Other Superpowers to add to your Self-compassion

Self-compassion becomes even more effective when we combine it with other things!

Sleep

Try and get lots of sleep, especially when you're working hard on something. Sleep will help you feel rested enough to do the best you can.

Diet

Eat plenty of fruits and vegetables and try to stay away from too many sugary drinks. The goodness in fruits and vegetables will give your superpower a boost and keep you focused.

Get Moving

Being active is an amazing way to stay positive and to keep unhealthy perfectionism at bay. Try and ride a bike or kick a ball around for at least ten minutes a day.

Stretching

Keeping our bodies loose helps our mind function better. Whenever you play sports or after you've been sitting for a long time, always loosen up the body with some stretches.

Routine

Many perfectionists find benefit in establishing a routine they use every day. This helps them know what's coming next, which helps them stay calm and focused.

Breath Routine

We learned the importance of breathing in Jack's story. Practicing our breathing even when we're not upset helps get us in the right mindset to do well.

Meditation & Yoga

Meditation and Yoga are powerful ways to focus the mind. To learn about them and to watch some cool videos that you can join in with, visit my friend Jaime at *www.cosmickids.com*

CP SAYS...

Congratulations! You now have your very own SELF-COMPASSION SUPERPOWER to use against your unhealthy perfectionism. You now know how it can help you and when to can use it, and if you forget, you can always come back to the book and remind yourself!

Trying to be the best you can be in everything you do is a wonderful quality but remember to be kind to yourself as you go along. Forgive yourself when you make mistakes, remind yourself daily of what makes you unique and special, and try to love yourself as much as you love other people.

Remember: self-compassion isn't just for kids!

Keep practicing it as you grow up. Many adults use self-compassion to manage their perfectionism, and the exercises and techniques you've learned in this book will help you for many years to come.

You are an insanely capable and wonderful human-being, and you deserve to be happy. Practice self-compassion regularly to keep your unhealthy perfectionism at bay, and if you need help, ask for it.

For more great ways to help your perfectionism and to visit the store, ask your mom, dad or guardian if you can visit *www.captain-perfection.com*

You're awesome, and it's been a pleasure helping you!

Captain Perfection

Dear grown-ups,

Thank you for giving your child the opportunity to learn more about their perfectionism! Every young perfectionist deserves to be happy and successful, and those who develop effective management techniques for their perfectionism early in life are the ones best placed to thrive.

To ensure your child can easily connect with the contents of this book, I've chosen to illustrate perfectionism in its simplest form. In reality, perfectionism is a vast and complicated subject with numerous definitions, and further reading and investigation is encouraged and advised.

The management techniques presented here are based on my own experiences and extensive research on the subject. Whilst I'm certain that the reader will benefit greatly from these offerings, I am not a trained psychologist. If your child continues to struggle with perfectionism after reading this book, you may wish to consult a professional who can help you further.

As your child begins to develop and embrace their own methods to cope with perfectionism, they will continue to rely on your support. Whilst this book is a personal learning experience for your child, parents will also benefit from reading it, and those that do may find themselves better positioned to help with their child's development.

If you are a perfectionist yourself, try to remember that children learn from what they see. Steering your young perfectionist away from obvious perfectionistic traits is a valuable starting point in their journey to a healthier life, and watching you be open to mistakes and less demanding of perfection in general lifts a huge weight from their shoulders.

More specific approaches will be helpful too; trying to stay calm when they have their perfectionistic episodes; having open conversations with them on how to deal with anxious thoughts; laughing at your own imperfections; not focusing too much on results; teaching them to break big projects into smaller pieces; etc.

Above all, teach them that *they are enough* — irrespective of what they achieve — and help them instill that belief. The growth from that standpoint alone will be huge.

Young perfectionists are wonderful souls but complicated people. You have my upmost respect for everything you do for them, and I'm always here to help where I can.

Visit *www.captain-perfection.com* for more self-compassion resources, and to visit the store.

CP

About the Author

Julian is a British author, consultant, and speaker, and has been a perfectionist for over forty years.

His adaptive perfectionism helped him become the Music Director for the Broadway musical *Hamilton* in the U.S. and played a considerable role in his fortune to travel the world with his work and establish three successful businesses in the creative sector.

His maladaptive perfectionism has not been so kind! Years of stress related to fear of failure in performance, low self-esteem and a bullying inner critic took its toll in 2017 when Julian experienced a heart attack aged just 43. This health scare prompted extensive research into perfectionism, the results of which now provide the foundation of his work.

Realizing that much of his experience with maladaptive perfectionism could have been avoided with more knowledge of the subject in childhood, Julian created Captain Perfection to inspire young perfectionists to develop robust and healthy management techniques for their perfectionism early on in life. The importance of self-compassion is central to his message and integral to his work with older perfectionists and companies that employ them.

He lives with his wife, Lisa, and dog, Ollie in California. Please visit *www.julianreeve.com* for more information.